Something To Know

Losing the Image of God/
Tithing and God's Recall

Rev. Conrad C. Henry Sr.

SOMETHING TO KNOW
Losing the Image of God/Tithing and God's Recall

Rev. Conrad C. Henry Sr.

ARPress
ILLUMINATING IDEAS
EMPOWERING VOICES

ARPress
45 Dan Road Suite 15
Canton MA 02021
  Hotline: 1(888) 821-0229
  Fax: 1(508) 545-7580

Ordering Information:
Quantity sales. Special discounts are available on quantity purchases by corporations, associations, and others. For details, contact the publisher at the address above.

Printed in the United States of America.

ISBN-13:   Softcover   979-8-89676-387-1
             eBook   979-8-89676-388-8

Library of Congress Control Number: 2025919886

CONTENTS

MAN LOSING THE
IMAGE OF GOD

MAN LOSING THE IMAGE OF GOD

From the book of Genesis Chapter 1, In the beginning God created the heaven and the earth, (The earth is the Lord, and the fullness thereof; the world and they that dwell therein. Ps. 24:1;) the earth and everything in it is God's creations, so no man can be credited for it.

In the beginning, is the beginning of the Creation, not the beginning of God existent, for God was before the creation and is self-existing, no explanation needed.

Now that we have established and accepted that God is the creator of all things in heaven and earth;

For; (The heaven's declare the glory of God, and the firmament sheweth his handy work. Ps. 19:1) all things were created by the power of God's word, (Let there be, and there it was.;)

The Plan for Man:

When it comes to the creation of man, it becomes personal; Let us make man, man has become his personal creation, hands on, which created a relationship and fellowship between God and man.

Genesis 1:26; And God said, let us make man in our own Image, after our likeness, (The plurality of us and our, can only be refer to the Father, Son, and Spirit; Jn.1:1,2;)

Genesis 1:27; So God created man in his own Image; The Image of God is the characteristic's of God. The Spiritual man; The Righteous man; The Holy Man; is the Image of God created he him, (male and female) created he them.

The species is man, the gender is male and female. (Their task was to multiply and replenish the earth). The male carries the seeds, the female deliver the seeds.

Every man (male and female) are in the population of man from creations.

The Lord God said let us make man in our own image, and likeness, what is God's Image and likeness?

I believe the Image of God is Spirit; Holiness and Righteousness.

(God is a Spirit, and they that worship him, must worship him in spirit and truth Jn. 4:24).

Holiness, (without which no man shall see God, Heb. 12:14b)

Righteousness, (Righteous art thou, O Lord, Ps. 119:137a.);

And his Likeness is; His Beauty, Will, Love and the ability to be Creative, etc, etc.

Every man (male or female) God created is Beautiful, there is no flaws in them; before Adam sin, but Adam sin contaminated them.

Every man (male or female) were given a Will of their own, which give them a right to make their own choices between good and evil.

Every man (male or female} are capable of Love, which is of a godly nature, to Love someone or something.

Every man (male or female) were given a purpose, and are creative in some sort of way.

Male and Female:

God has created all the creatures of the earth, and the fowl's of the air, and the fish's of the sea in pairs, male and female, for the multiplication of each species on earth, air and sea.

The Lord God, gave man the same task, so he make them male and female, for the multiplication of the human race. It cannot be any other way.

Two male cannot have babies, neither can two females have babies. It takes a male and a female to have babies for the population of the human race. It is so ordained by God himself.

Genesis 1:28; And God blessed them, and God said unto them, be fruitful and multiply and replenish the earth. (And God said unto them, Them plural, they need each other for the task).

Genesis 2:7; And the Lord God formed man of the dust of the ground, (gives man a connection with the earth) and breathed into his nostril the breath of life, and man became a living soul, a connection with God, with a Body, Soul and Spirit. The creation of man from the earth, gives man the attachment and authority over all the creation, which God entrusted unto him.

God Provides Man with a Home and Provisions:

Genesis 2:8; And the Lord God planted a garden eastward in Eden (First given location), and there he put the man whom he had formed.

This garden was man's home, he was suppose to eat, sleep and live without the rest of the animals, even though he had access to all the animals.

Genesis 2:9; And out of the ground made the Lord God to grow every tree that is pleasant to the sight and good for food; the tree of life also in the mist of the garden, and the tree of knowledge of good and evil.

Note here, every tree that was planted in the garden including the tree of life is pleasant to the sight and good for food. But, the tree of knowledge of good and evil which was in the garden, was the only tree in the garden that was off limit.

Man could have eaten of the Tree of Life, which was the fruit of the

Spirit, and the fruit of the Spirit consist of these fruits; Love, joy, peace, long-suffering, gentleness, goodness, faith, meekness and temperance.

The tree of good and evil which were forbidden, because its main ingredients were full of wickedness, and produce fleshly desire's such as; adultery, fornication, uncleanness, hatred, lasciviousness, Idolatry, witchcraft, variance, emulations, wrath, strife, sedition's, heresies, envying and revelings., which is all poisonous and deadly.

Man's First Instruction:

Genesis 2:15-17; And the Lord God took the man (the male known as Adam) put him into the garden of Eden to dress it and keep it. V. 16; And the Lord God commanded the man (The male) saying of every tree of the garden thou mayst freely eat. Adam was free to eat of every tree including the tree of life. V. 17; But of the tree of knowledge of good and evil, thou shall not eat of it; (Warning before Destruction) for in the day that thou eatest thereof thou shalt surely die.

The instruction was not grievous, but was precise, you eat of this tree you die. The fruit of the tree of knowledge of good and evil, which some call an apple, is more deadly than any apple. It fruits is the fruits of sin, and death. (God intention here was for man not to have any knowledge of good and evil, but remain in his image of innocent). Eating from the tree of knowledge of good and evil carries a penalty, (death).

The death here is not referring only to the physical death, but also to the spiritual death as well; which makes man would die to the Image of God. Though the fellowship and the relationship between God and man was broken, man could regain this fellowship and relationship thought prayer and sacrifice to God on his own, but not in his Image, only through the ultimate sacrifice of Jesus Christ his only begotten Son, the Image of God can be restored to man, and man must accepted the sacrifice that Jesus Christ made on the cross.

The Female:

Genesis 2:18, Introduces the plan for the female and her purpose; And the Lord God said, it is not good that the man should be alone; I will make him an help meet for him.

(An help meet for him, the female, not only for companionship and domestic purposes, but for the multiplications and replenish the earth.)

Man was given the authority to name all of God creations, Genesis 2:19,20;

Genesis 2:21,22,23; And the Lord God caused a deep sleep to fall upon Adam and he slept; and he took one of his ribs, and closed up the flesh instead thereof; it was the first surgery performed on man by God.

V. 22; And the rib, which the Lord God had taken from man (Male) made he a woman (Female, a man with a womb) and brought her to Adam.

V. 23; And Adam said, this is now bone of my bones, and flesh of my flesh, (A relationship) she shall be called Woman because she was taken out of man. (Note here; that, this is the only time that a man gives birth through the extraction of the rib by God, for the woman was taken out of him by operation of his creator, he is the potter, we are the clay).

The woman was taken out of the man, which started the chain connection of all human being, regardless of race, color or creed, we are all connected to Adam, and Adam connected to the earth.

The First Marriage and Vow:

Genesis 2:24,25; Therefore, shall a man leave his father and mother, and shall cleave unto his wife: and they shall be one flesh. There is no room for two of the same gender to get married, for a man (male) leave his father and mother, and cleave to his wife. (not his husband).

Everything is going according to God's plan, man has been created, given a home, given authority over all the creatures on earth, even name them; given instructions how to live a long and prosperous life, given a wife and having a relationship and fellowship with the Lord God himself. And are still in the Image of God.

The Fall of Man and Losing the Image of God:

Genesis 3:1; Now the serpent was more subtil (Crafty) than any beast of the field which the Lord God had made. And he said unto the woman, Yea, hath God said, Ye shall not eat of every tree of the garden?

I believe the temptation of the woman (Eve) not yet named, were not in the garden of Eden their home, for Adam would have known about it, so she was away from her home and the security of Adam.

Note:

(1) She should have been by her husband side;

(2) She shouldn't be having any conversation with any of the beast of the field;

(3) The formation of the serpent question to get information should have caught her attention, "God said ye shall not eat of every tree in the garden?" she should have known that was a lie and walk away.

(4) It is obvious that the serpent didn't know which tree either, or its location God had warn them about. He was seeking information.

(5) She gave the information the serpent was seeking for.

Genesis 3:2; And the woman said unto the serpent, we may eat of the fruit of the trees of the garden:

V. 3 But of the fruit of the tree which is in the mist of the garden (location given), God hath said, ye shall not eat of it, neither shall ye touch it, lest ye die.

(Chapter 2:16,17; "And the Lord God commanded the man, saying, of every tree of the garden thou mayest freely eat: V. 18, But of the tree of knowledge of good and evil, thou shalt not eat of it: for the day that thou eatest thereof thou shalt surely die.") The woman here added another condition to the danger of the tree, even if you only touch it you'll die.

The serpent responded to her, with a lie that sound like the truth.

V. 4, And the serpent said unto her, Ye shall not surely die.

The art of deception was instigated by the serpent;

V. 5, For God doth know that in that day ye eat thereof, then your eyes shall be opened, and ye shall be as gods, knowing good and evil. There were some truth in that saying their eyes will be open to know good and evil, but the lie was they won't die, and they would become a god.

The woman knew the truth, but listen to the lies;

V. 6b, she took of the fruit thereof and did eat, and gave also unto her husband with her, and he did eat.

The serpent did not deceive the man, but the woman, the man had the option here not to partake of eating the fruit the woman gave to him, he had firsthand information about eating of that fruit, and the result of eating of that fruit is forbidden. God himself had instructed him. The entire world population was in Adam and depended on Adam's decision. That's why we inherited Adam sin. Every conception of a child, whether a day or a month old is in the plan of God and was in Adam, and have a right to live.

The question asked here is, was Adam afraid of losing the only woman he knows, knowing what it was to be without a companion? Was it because she was bone of his bones, and flesh of his flesh? Or his love for her, he was willing to die with her and plunge all of mankind unto death? Just as God so love the world, that he gave his only begotten Son, as a living sacrifice to save the world and give everlasting life to all that believed on Him (Jn. 3:16).

Their Eyes were Opened:

Gen. 3:7; And the eyes of them both were opened, and they knew that they were naked; (Their clothing of innocence were removed, and for the first time they saw themselves naked and were ashamed of what they see). And they sewed fig leaves together, and made themselves aprons. Eating of the fruit of good and evil, had revealed to them something they were not aware of, and try to cover it up. Even in today's world, we will try do anything to cover up our sins.

Man Lost the Image and Fellowship with God:

Gen.3:8; And they heard the voice of the Lord God walking in the garden in the cool of the day; and Adam and his wife hid themselves from the presence of the Lord God amongst the trees of the garden Adam and his wife (She wasn't name Eve as yet), knew what they have done, and went and hid themselves, they heard his voice as they accustom too, but it was different, not joyful, but angry, they have broken the trust, by been disobedient; the fellowship they had with the Lord God before they eat of the tree of good and evil was over, they couldn't face the Lord God anymore, because they were ashamed, so they went and hide themselves, (sometimes, if it were possible, we feel like hiding ourselves for the things we have done, but you can't hide from God).

Gen. 3:9; And the Lord God called unto Adam, and said unto him, Where art thou? (I believed God knew where Adam and his wife was, but Adam and his wife heard his voice, but didn't knew where he was?)

Gen. 3:10, And he said, I heard thy voice in the garden, and I was afraid, because I was naked; and I hid myself. Adam, had just confess of his predicament knowing what he had done, and he could not face his master in his state he was in, so he could hear his voice, but he couldn't see his face; Adam had not just lost fellowship with God, but also the Image of God; No man born of a woman after Adam sin, were born in the Image of God ever since Adam sin, but in the Image of Adam.

Gen. 5:3; And Adam lived a hundred and thirty years, and begat a son in his own likeness after his image; and called his name Seth.

Only Jesus Christ born of a woman, were born in the Image of God, through the virgin birth.

(Matt. 1:23; Behold, a virgin shall be with child, and shall bring forth a son, and they shall call his name Emmanuel, which interpreted is, God with us.).

Man has lost the Image of God, and the relationship and fellowship was broken. Because of sin, there is no Intimacy and relationship between God and man. God loves us and wanted to restore us in his Image, but only through his son Christ Jesus, (Col. 1:15 Who is the image of the invisible God, the first born of every creature:)

Naked before God:

Gen. 3:11; And he said, who told thee that thou was naked? (There wasn't anyone else to tell him, but the sin he has committed and the guilt reveals his nakedness.) Hast thou eaten of the tree, whereof I command thee that thou shouldest not eat? Adam did not answer yes, or no; the *man*, went directly to the blame game, and try to wiggle out of his responsibility. It's not my fault. No one had to tell Adam, they were naked; their eyes were open and for the first time they saw their own nakedness, and they were ashamed of what they saw.

Gen. 3:12; And the man said, the woman whom thou gave to be with me, she gave me of the tree and I did eat. There is no evidence here which say that the woman forces him, or plea with him to eat of the fruit, but it seem to be voluntary.

Gen. 3:13; And the Lord God said unto the woman, What is this that thou hast done? And the woman said, The serpent beguiled me, and I did eat. They knew that they were guilty even though they tried to blame each other. We all know when we have done something wrong even if we say someone else encourage us to do so, we inherit it from

Adam, by him eating of the tree of knowledge, of good and evil.

Gen. 3:14,15; The serpent was punished, and his punishment was a cursed, to crawl on its belly and dust was its food for the rest of its life. From now on you and the woman will be enemies, and her offspring shall crush his head, and he shall bruised his heel.

V. 15 was of the Messianic Prophecies, the Messiah was bruised on the cross on Mount Calvary.

Gen. 3:16; Unto the woman he said, I will greatly multiply thy sorrow and thy conception; in sorrow thou shall bring forth children; and thy desire shall be to thy husband, and he shall rule over thee.

It appears here, that child bearing should be painless to the woman at the time of conception, with some or none discomfort, but now, because she listen to the serpent, child bearing would be painful with suffering, that was the punishment for the woman.

Gen. 3:17; And unto Adam he said, because thou hast hearkened unto the voice of thy wife, and has eaten of the tree of which I commanded thee, saying, thou shalt eat not of it; cursed is the ground for thy sake; in sorrow shalt thou eat of till all the days of thy life;

Because thou hast hearkened (Listen) to the voice of thy wife; (the voice of thy wife, the voice of thy mother, father, brother, friend or any voice that encourage you to do whatever you know is wrong; you and you alone must accept the consequence and not blaming another, for the choices you make in life.

Cursed is the Ground:

Gen. 3:18; Thoms also and thistles shall it bring forth to thee; and thou shalt eat of the herb of the field.

Adam disobedience did not only affect himself, but also all of mankind, creatures of the land, sea and air; for everything was taken out of the ground, and Adam has a connection to the ground, for he was made out of the ground, everything that created was for the comfort of man; and so he gave man authority over all creature's and to name them.

The earth was commanded to bring forth thorns and thistles; not only did the earth bring forth thorns and thistles, and whatever it desires, such as earthquakes, volcanoes, flies,, roaches, mosquitoes, and anything that will makes man uncomfortable for his sin, the beast of the field, the bird's of the air, the and the fishes of the sea, had turned against man who once has authority over them, man has become their enemies.

Because of Adam sin, the air also produces hurricanes, tornadoes, and strong winds; the sea produces tsunami, storms, high waves, etc. etc.

Gen. 3:22; And the Lord God said, Behold , the man is become as one of us, to know good and evil. (God here acknowledge that man now know what's good and evil is, which make him responsibly for his own actions) I believed it was God intentions for the man to remain in his innocent states, and wouldn't have to choose any which way, but the man hearken to the voice of his wife, and the wife hearken to voice of the serpent, and man hides when he heard the voice of the Lord God.

And now, lest he put forth his hand, and take also of the tree of life, and eat, and live forever. (Because of the man ability to choose, if it were possible, that man could get to the tree of life and eat of that fruit, man would have live in that sinful states for the rest of his life and would never die).

Christ Jesus, the only begotten Son of God, who was there in the plan of all creations, and also in the plan of redemption of man, if man messes up.

The Lord God knew that Adam could sin, because of his will, and notify him of the danger of eating of the tree of good and evil, but God did not prejudge Adam, but put all in prospective and preparation for the salvation of man his most valuable and unique possession on earth, one that he created with his own hand, if he sin.

Christ Jesus, the only begotten Son of God, represent the tree of life, his death on the cross, hanging from a tree, he could boldly say to the repented thief beside him today thou shalt be with me in paradise. The garden of Eden, which is paradise, has been regam.

I believed that every born again believer's that die in Christ Jesus goes back to the garden of Eden, and not to heaven, as some had stated.

While man covered himself with fig leaves to cover his shame, and the fig leaves will rot, God gave them a more appropriate covering; more durable, and will last longer than the fig leaves; a covering of skin.

Gen. 3:23; Therefore, the Lord God sent him forth from the garden of Eden, (Man's first eviction) to till the ground from whence he was taken; Provision was made for him while he was in the garden, now he must provides for himself and his wife, by the sweat of his face is the only way he can eat.

Gen. 3:24; So he drove out the man; and he placed at the east of the garden of Eden, Cherubims, and a flaming sword which turned every way, to keep the way of the tree of life.

It appears here, that there is only one entrance into the garden, where the tree of life is planted, and it is well protected. And guarded by the Cherubims with flaming swords, so that no man can just walk in, and eat of the tree of life. Even today, some believes that they can just walk in the kingdom of God any which way because they attended a religious organization and the have given a lot of money, but Jesus Christ is the only way to the kingdom of God, that's why he could say to the thief on the cross, today thou shall be with me in paradise.

Adam Sin Produce the Evidence of Good and Evil:

Gen. 4:1; And Adam knew Eve his wife; and she conceived, and bare Cain, and said, I have gotten a man from the Lord.

2a; And she again bare his brother Abel, the brother's represent good and evil. Cain represent evil, and Abel represent good, and the tree of good and evil has been established. And so dwelleth in every man (male and female) good and evil.

May the good part of man overcome the evil part, and God help us all. Amen.

Adam sin brings forth death to all, both man and beast. Nothing would have died if it were not for Adam disobedience.

Adam sin also bring death to the Spiritual man and the physical man.

Jesus Christ physical death, brings life to the Spiritual man, that's why ye must be born again, for the spiritual man to be resurrected in you.

Every man according to God's plan in the beginning were created in God's Image, but after Adam sin, no man are born in the Image of God, except for Jesus Christ, who was born of a Virgin Birth.

Matt. 1:23; Behold a virgin shall be with child, and shall bring forth a son, and they shall call his name Emmanuel, which being interpreted is, God with us.

Luke 1:34; Then said Mary unto the angel, How shall this be, seeing I know not a man. Mary pregnancy were not contaminated by sinful man, because her pregnancy was by the Holy Ghost.

In the eyes of God you are special; you are wonderfully made.

If this world were a Pottery, God is the potter and you are the clay, whom he formed and fashion with his own hands and in his own likeness.

In the eyes of God, you are not too small or big, short or tall, skinny or fat, black or white, red or yellow. You may feel unloved, but God love you, with his love for you through Jesus Christ his only begotten Son; you try to push Him away, but he won't leave you alone, because he loves you just as you are. He Love You.

If this world were a Painter's Canvas, then God is the only Artist that paints such beautiful scenery, and a living portrait of you, that move and breathe and have it being. And in the eyes of God you are one of His precious master piece, and not just a piece of canvas with a painting, but one that is sign, seal and framed with the precious blood of his Son Christ Jesus.

If this world were a Botanical Garden, God is the biologist, in the eyes of God, you are one of the plants he grafted into the tree of Life. And are preserved and groomed, which he manicure with his Love, and life eternal.

If this world were a Zoo, then God is the Zoologist, a specialist that studies you, your behavior, characteristic, and divinely apply with kindness and love all your necessary needs.

If this world were a field of Jewels, then God is the Jeweler, and in his eyes you are unique and precious, if you are broken only he can fix you like no other can. He designs and fashion you in beauty, and adorn you with his Grace, and place you with his collections of diamonds, rubies, jasper, emeralds, gold and pearls, to name a few of his treasures, you are most precious to him.

If this world were a Museum, then God is the one that design such awesome display of you, not as an artifact that cannot move, but as one that is alive in his collections. In the eyes of God, you are one of his most precious in his gallery of exhibits.

If this world were a Vineyard, God is the Husbandman, in his eyes you are a branch of his vine, and he expected you to be fruitful, and if you don't, he will prune you, dig around you, fertilized you so that you can bring forth much fruit. He is just that patient with you.

If the world seem to be in darkness, and the sun and moon cannot illuminates it, in the eyes of God you are that light that shines into darkness, that lead those that are in darkness to that great Light (Jesus Christ) So, let your light so shine before men, that they may see your good works, and glorify your Father in heaven.

God is Ready to Restore Man Back to His Image:

John 3:16,17; For God so loved the world, that he gave his only begotten Son, that whosoever believeth in him should not perish, but have everlasting life.

For God sent not his Son into the world to condemn the world; but that the world through him might saved.

In a world that is full of great buildings, palaces, castles, and cathedrals that are made to accommodate, kings and royalties, popes and presidents, there are no building large enough to contain the God of Creation, yet there is room in your heart, if you let him in, for he said in (Revelation 3:20) Behold, I stand at the door, and knock, if any man hear my voice, and open the door, I will come in and sup with him, and he with me.

All you have to do right now, where ever you are; Repent of your sins, acknowledge you are a sinner and in need of a Savior, which is Christ Jesus, confess and accept Jesus Christ as your Lord, Savior and Redeemer, get baptize, and thou shall be save.

GLORY BE TO GOD.

GOD'S RECALL

GOD'S RECALL

Manufacturers had recalled may of their products, such as cars and trucks, toys, food products and many other things, because of defects and its dangerous to the public, any one with such recall items must returned such items, for a refund or exchange. Items is recalled because of some defects were found and must be rectified before someone gets hurt. If you refuses to return such item, whatever happen to you will be your fault and no one else can be blame for your decision of not returning this product.

God has been calling men and women to return to Him ever since the fall of man because of Adam sin. Adam sin plunges the entire human race into a state of defect, so man remain in an malfunction state of life, everyone is recalled by God because all have sin, and come short of the glory of God.

In the book of Jeremiah 3:22a God said Return, Joel 2:12; Therefore also now, saith the Lord, tum ye even to me with all your heart. God , is not willing that any (means any) should perish, but that all should come to repentance, for he is gracious and merciful, slow to anger, and of great kindness. there are many things that we have done that God hates, here are some of them on the list, Proverbs 6:16-19; These six things doth the Lord hate: yea, seven are an abomination unto him: (1) A proud look, (2) a lying tongue, an (3) hands that shed innocent blood, (4) heart that deviseth wicket imaginations, (5) feet that is swift in running to mischief, (6) a false witness that speaketh lies, (7) and he that soweth discord among brethren. The apostle Paul in the New testament added at least three more things that God hates, (8) an itching Ears, only listen to bad news and gossips, 2 Timothy 4:3-4; For the time will come when they will not endure sound doctrine: but after their own lust shall they heap to themselves teachers, having itching ears; and shall tum away their ears from the truth, (9) Lustful eyes; 1 John 2:15-16; Love not the world, neither the thing that are in the world. If any man love the world, the love of the Father is not in him. For all that is in the world, the lust of the flesh, and the lust of the eyes (a proud look) and the pride of life. (10) A defiled body, Romans 1:24; Wherefore God also gave them over to uncleanness through the lust of their own hearts, to dishonor their own bodies between themselves:

These 10 things are some of the things that defiles a man, and requires him for the need to return to God to be renewed by the blood of Jesus Christ.

2 Corinthians 5:17; Therefore if any man (means any Man, male or female) be in Christ, him/her is a new creature: old things are passed away; behold, all things are new. And God had regenerated the old spirit of man, and gave him/her a new spirit of life. Lets take a look at these 10 things God hated, one by one briefly;

1) <u>A Proud Look;</u> pride is the first, for we have an attitude about ourselves, that over value ourselves, and under values everybody else, sometimes we even believes that we are God gifts to the world, and the other person doesn't matter, most man, male /female look down on others, because of their family status, being rich, a little more educated, their beautiful physical looks, not knowing that beauty comes from within. Some believed that they are the best thing that happen to their mother or father, husband or wife, and the world revolved around them. Proverbs 16:18; Pride goeth before destruction, and an haughty spirit before a fall. Love your neighbors and be ye kind one to another.

2) <u>A Lying Tongue;</u> the book of James 1:26, says, if any man among you seem to be religious, and bridleth not his tongue, but deceiveth his own heart, this man religion is vain; James 3:6; And the tongue is a fire, a world of iniquity: so is the tongue among our members, that it defileth the whole body, and setteth on fire the course of nature; and it is set on fire of hell. Death and Life are in the power of the tongue (Proverbs 18:21).
The tongue is a powerful member of the body, it's the only member that can bless and curse at the same time. These speech

pattern of the tongue that can be of help. The controlled, the caring, the conniving, and the careless tongue languages.

(a) The Controlled Tongue; Thinks before it speak, and know when silence is best, and gives wise advises.

(b) The Caring Tongue; It will tells you the truth every time even if you don't want to hear it, because it cares.

(c) The Conniving Tongue; This speech will tell you one thing, and means another, it is filled with rumors, gossip's, wrong intensions and motives, swelling words and twisted truths, and fill with lies, know how to avoid it.

(d) The Careless Tongue, it speaks lies continually, and curses all the time, quick tempered when not believed, someone says, half the trouble in the world today, comes from people who don't know what to say, and the tongue can light a fire in a moment.

3) <u>Hands that Shed Innocent Blood</u>; there are those who are so blood thirsty to hurt others, that they don't care who they hurt, even if that person is innocents. They look for trouble at any cost, even if it means murder. They are on duty daily looking for blood, and can't wait for the opportunity to hurt someone.

4) <u>A Heart that Deviseth Wicked Imagination</u>; It's a well known fact, that the heart is deceitful above all things, and desperately wicked. Who can know it? Jer. 17:9; the heart can laugh with you, hug and kiss you, called you friend, make you feel secured and still stab you in the back, and set traps for your downfall.

5) <u>Feet that be Swift in Running to Mischief</u>: some can hardly wait to run and hear the bad news of your neighbors, your feet will take you places you should not be in the first place, but you love mischief. Some will even twist the truth to satisfied their ego, that's how much they love mischief.

6) <u>A False Witness</u>: weren't there, but can tell the story better than the eye witness, a false witness will twist everything someone

told them about the situation to suit their imagination, and if been paid will give you a better version of what happen that didn't happen.

7) <u>He that Soweth Discord among Brethren</u>: these are they who hates to see others get along, they will dig-up, rig-up and produce some kind of a story to disrupt a good relationship between friends, Husband and Wife, Brothers and Sisters and Families and neighbor's, at work, homes schools even in the churches.

8) <u>Itching Ears</u>: For the time will come when they will not endure sound doctrine; but after their own lust shall they heap to themselves teachers, having itching ears; And they shall turn away their ears from the truth, and shall turned unto fable (2 Tim 4:3,4), there are those who no longer wanted to hear the truth about the good old Gospel of Jesus Christ, so they are willing to hear fables (makeup stories) and false hope teachers, they are looking for someone to make them feel good in their sinful states, and giving them false hope.

9) <u>Lustful Eyes</u>: Love not the world, neither the things that are in the world. If any man loved the world, the love of the Father is not in him. For all that is in the world, the lust of the flesh, and the lust of the eyes, and pride of life, is not of the Father, but of the world (1 John 2:15,16). The eyes, the flesh and the pride of life, work as one unit of the body inherited by every man, and can destroy any man, with the eyes that is filled with lust, no man can lust about what they cannot see, the lust of the eyes is fill with covetousness, and the flesh with pride enhance it. The lustful eyes see it, wants it, and it has to be bigger and better than anyone else, and never satisfied, contentment is not the life style of the lustful eyes; it drives us to get that which we cannot afford.

10) <u>Defiled Body</u>: there are those who may think that God our creator has made a mistake's with them, for they feel like a man trap in a woman's body, or a woman trap in a man's body,

not knowing that the sin's in us, our flesh gives the species the desires to become what ever we wanted to be; a thief, a liar, a murderer, a whore or what ever, that choice you have to make for yourself, for God doesn't make it for you. For God said, I set before you Life an Death, Blessing and Curse, therefore choose life, but He does not force you. Again the choice is yours, so what you have become is what you wanted to be. The apostle Paul stated it this way in the book of Romans 1:24, 26,27 Wherefore God also gave them up to uncleanness through the lust of their own hearts, to dishonor their own bodies between themselves: V. 26; For this cause God gave them unto vile affections: for even their women did change the natural use into that which is against nature: V. 27; And likewise also the men, leaving the natural use of the women, burned in their lust one toward another; men with men working that is unseemly, and receiving in themselves that recompence of their error which was meet. So you see, when they knew of God they glorified Him not as their God.

God Recalls Us:

For the Lord your God is gracious and compassionate. He will not tum his face from you if you return to him. 2 Chronicles 30:9h

Let the wicked forsake their ways and the unrighteous their thoughts. Let them tum to the Lord, and he will have mercy on them, and to our God, for he will freely pardon. Isaiah 55:7

Promised A New Heart and A New Spirit:

A new heart also will I will give to you, and a new spirit will I put within you: and I will take away the stony heart out of your flesh, and I will give an heart of flesh. Ezekiel 36:26.

Given a New Name:

The nation shall see your righteousness, and all the kings your glory, and you shall be called by a new name that the mouth of the Lord will give. Isaiah 62:2

Man Needed a Fixup:

Man returning to God, will be given a new make-over. Therefore if any man be in Christ, he is a new creature: old things are passed away; behold all things are become new. 2 Corinthians 5:17

He gave me a new attitude of life, now I can be humble.

He gave me a new tongue, now I can talk right and speak the truth.

He gave me new hands, now I can lift them up in praise to Him.

He gave me a new heart, now I can love everybody.

He gave me new feet, now I am running for my Jesus.

I am a true witness, I can tell the world of His goodness to me.

He makes me to know peace, and sow it with joy among my brethren.

I now know the truth, for the truth had set me free.

He removed the lust from my eyes, now I can see the beauty of his creations with appreciation.

He redeemed me from my sins mind, body and soul and I am walking in the light of his goodness and grace.

Returned to God, and He will return to you.

Just present your body a living sacrifice, holy and acceptable unto God which is a reasonable service. May God be praise.

TITHING/OFFERING

TITHING/OFFERING

Understanding the Concept of Tithe and Offering:

Tithing a 10% of all one possess, a requirement for the Jewish Nation, as a contribution to the work of the ministries, and an inheritance for the Tribe of the Levites and Priest. With a providential clause to take care of the widows, orphans, and strangers. It is not mandatory in the New Testament Church.

I am not trying to confuse or discourage any one not to give to the church, for the church needs every financial help that can be given to it in this world today.

The Introduction of Tithing or a Tenth:

Gen.14:18-20; And Melchizedek king of Salem brought forth bread and wine: and he was the priest of the most high God.

V. 19; And he blessed him, and said, blessed be Abram of the most high God, possessor of heaven and earth:

V. 20; And blessed be the most high God, which hath delivered thine enemies into thy hand. And he gave him tithes of all.

The First Account of Tithe, and Voluntary:

Abram, had just defeated three kings, and was on his way back to his home in the land of Mam're which is in Hebron. When he was met by king Melchizedek, who brought bread and wine for him and his soldiers, and in congratulations of their victory. Melchizedek, king and high priest of the most high God in the land of Salem bless Abram. In gratitude; Abram present an offering to him Melchizedek.

Abram, gave him tithes or a tenth of all the spoils he had gotten in victory over the enemies. Dedicated to the most high God. It is fitting that we should express our thankfulness to the most high God by giving some special gift in honor to God. Jesus Christ our great Melchizedek (Heb. 7:5-9) is to have homage done him, and to be humbly acknowledge by every one of us as our King and Priest; and not only the tithe of all, but all we have must be surrendered and given up to him.

Tithes or a Tenth with Conditions:

Gen. 28:20-22; And Jacob vowed a vow, saying, If God will be with me, and will keep me in the way that I go, and will give me bread to eat, and raiment to put on.

V. 21; So that I come again to my father's house in peace; then shall the Lord be my God:

V. 22; And this stone, which I have set for a pillar, shall be God's house: and of all that thou shalt give me I will surely give the tenth unto thee.

Sometimes, we find ourselves in situation's whereby we makes vow, or promises that we only intended to keep if everything goes alright; and sometimes it doesn't.

Jacob vowed a vow, Jacob's modesty and great moderation in his desire to give a tenth of his substance to God. He will cheerfully be content himself with bread to eat and clothes to wear. Jacob piety and his regard to God, which appears here, was his desires for God to be with him, provides for him food and clothes, and his divine protection to bring him back to his father's house.

The Importance of Tithing:
Lev. 27:30-33

A law concerning tithes which were paid for the service of God before the law, as appears by Abraham, Gen. 14:20; and Jacob promise to God, Gen. 28:22;

Lev. 27:30; And all the tithe of the land, whether of the seed of the land, or of the fruit of the tree, is the Lord's: it is Holy unto the Lord.

It is here appointed, that they should pay tithes of all; whether its from the land or the fruit of the trees, or the first fruit of the animals. We are taught here to honor God with our substance, Prov. 3:9-10, Honor the Lord with thy substance, and with the first fruits of all thine increase.

V. 31; And if a man will at all redeem (or buy back) ought of his tithes, he shall add therein the fifth (5th) part thereof.

God taught the Israelite's that when they made a vow to him that they must not go back on it, for if they do, there is an increase of a fifth (5th) added to what ever they had vow.

Ecc. 5:4,5; when thou vowest a vow unto God, defer not to pay it, for he hath no pleasure in fools, pay that which thou hast vow.

V. 5; Better is it that thou shouldest not vow, than to vow and pay not.

Lev. 27:30-33 says that a tenth of all that the land produces is to be "Holy to the Lord." The underlying concept is that the tithe is "rent or lease" which Israel owes to God for the use of His land.

The Tithe Becomes an Inheritance for the Tribe of the Levites:

Num. 18:20-24

Num. 18:20; And the Lord spake unto Aaron. Thou shalt have no inheritance in their land, neither shalt thou have any part among them: I am thy part and thy inheritance among the children of Israel.

V. 21; And, behold, I have given the children of Levi all the tenth in Israel for an inheritance, for their service, even the service of the tabernacle of the congregation.

V. 22; Neither must the children of Israel henceforth come nigh themselves the tabernacle of the congregation, lest they bear sin, and die.

V. 23; But the Levites shall do the service of the tabernacle of the congregation, and they shall bear their iniquity: it shall be a statue for ever throughout your generations, that among the children of Israel they shall have no inheritance

V. 18:24; But the Tithes of the children of Israel, which they offer as an heave or waving offering unto the Lord, I have given to the Levites to Inherit: therefore I have said unto them, Among the children of Israel they shall have no inheritance.

All the tithes of the land were given to the Levites that were intended for the Lord, but by God's permission, it was given to them as their only inheritance in the land, their task is to take care of the services, and of the tabernacle.

The provision was made both for the Levites and the Priests, for they have no inheritance in the land. They must dwell in the city which were allowed them, but no ground for them to occupied.

Num. 18:20-24; tells us that the tithe was to be used to maintain the Levites, who would receive no tribal land when in Canaan for their inheritance.

When it comes to tithing in the New Testament church, the most used scripture by our Leader's today is Mal.3:8-10; Will a man rob God?

The Israelite's wasn't withholding their tithes and offering, but when they give they give their worst, God said through Malachi centuries later , calling on His people to obey the law of the tithe.

Mal. 3:10; Bring ye all the tithes into the storehouse, that there may be meat in mine house, and prove me now herewith, said the Lord of hosts, if I will not open you the windows of heaven, and pour you out a blessing , that there shall not be room enough to receive it.

Those who tithed not only kept a divine commandment, they also expressed confidence in God's ability to provide for them.

They weren't robbing God not by giving of the tenth, but were robbing God by giving of their worst.

The New Testament:
Offering/Freewill Offering:

When it comes to the New testament church, there is no passage found that imposes tithe as an obligation, or mandatory setting of tithing on Christians. Though there is a guided principle of giving in the church, and it should be considered as an freewill offering.

The New Testament Church begin its giving with a 100% of those who gives.

Acts 4:34-35; Neither was there any among them that lacked: for as many as were possessors of lands and houses sold them, and brought the prices of the things that were sold,

V. 35; And laid them down at the apostles feet: and distribution was made unto every man according as he had need.

I believed, every born again Christians, has a desire to give, and gives to the best of their ability, but the problem is, some feels guilty because they are not able to give as much as the other person or the require tenth imposed upon them by their leaders, and it makes them feels like they are robbing God, because when it comes to giving, all they can hear "will a man rob God." and not give as God has prosper you, and give it from your heart.

It is encouraged that every one should give to the house of God, as God has prosper them, regularly, and cheerfully, and not out of necessity, and should not be pressured to give; but should be taught on how to give. The church has need of money for its operational system in the world, and should also have a storehouse for the distributions to the poor, the widows and orphans. Its a missionary ministries. Giving to the church should be called a freewill offering and not tithing. For there is no set percentage on how much to give to it, and all should be given from the heart.

Tithing in the Old Testament:

Tithing is a commandment

Tithing is a tenth of all; first-fruit, first-produce; firstlings of the flocks and herd.

It's the reward or inheritance to the Levites for their service in the temple.

A tenth of the tenth was given to the Priest for their portion of their inheritance.

A special tenth was to be collected every third year for the poor and the needy.

Tithing is mandatory in the Old Testament.

Offering/Freewill Offering:
How One Should Give to the Church:

Freely; Luke 6:38, Give and it shall be given unto you, good measure, pressed down, and shaken together, and running over, shall men give into your bosom. For with the same measure that you mete withal it shall be measured to you again.

Regularly; 1 Cor. 16:2; Upon the first day of the week let every one of you lay by him in the store, as God hath prospered him.

Cheerfully; 2 Cor. 9:7; Every man according as he purposeth in his heart, so let him give, not grudging, or of necessity: for God loveth a cheerful giver.

Not Grudgingly; Acts 5:1–4; But a certain man named Ananias, with Sapphira his wife, sold a possession,

V. 2; And kept back part of the price, his wife also being privy to it, and brought a certain part, and laid it at the Apostles feet.

V. 3; But Peter said, Ananias why hath Satan filled thine heart to lie to the Holy Ghost, and to keep back part of the price of the land?

V. 4; Whiles it remained, was it not thine own? And after it was sold was it not in thine own power? Why hast thou conceived this thing in thine heart? Thou hast not lied unto men, but unto God.

The land was theirs, the money they sold it for was theirs, but they make a pledge to give it all, only to withhold a portion of it.

Your possession is in your hand to do whatever, or to give whatever, that power is in your hand, but whatever you give, give it from the heart. We must be careful with the vows we make.

The book of Ecclesiastes chap 5:4–5; teaches us; when thou vowest a vow unto God, defer not to pay it, for he hath no pleasure in fools.

V. 5; Better is it that thou shouldest not vow, than that shouldest vow and not pay.

You give because you are bless, so give to be a blessing to someone, so give;

Paul wrote to the church at Corinth; 1st Cor. 16:1-3; Now concerning the collection for the saints, as I have given order to the churches of Galatia, even so do.

V. 2; Upon the first day of the week let every one of you lay by him in store, as God hath prospered him, that there be no gathering when I come.

It appears here, that there was some confusion about the offering collected at the church in Corinth, and the distribution were not distributed as it should. He refer them to take pattern of them in Galatia, and do the same as they do.

It's imperative for the churches to collect the free will offering on the first day of the week, or any day that a freewill offering is given.

In the church, we only have one High Priest, in the person of our Lord and Savior Jesus Christ, and he was called after the order of Melchizedek; and not after the order of Aaron; (Heb. 7:12). V. 12; for the priesthood being changed, there is made of the necessity a change also of the law.

Give because you Love; 1st Cor. 13:3; And though I bestow all my goods to the poor, and though I give my body to be burned, and have not Love or charity, it profiteth me nothing.

Please don't be afraid to give to the church, weather a dime or a dollar, give it from your heart, and for the Love of Christ and the Church. Amen. To God be the Glory.